The OFFICIAL RUBBER CHICKEN PRACTICAL Jokes & Riddles Book

By
Chris Tait

Copyright © 1999 Kidsbooks, Inc.
3535 West Peterson Avenue
Chicago, IL 60659

Visit us at www.kidsbooks.com
Volume discounts available for group purchases.

Funny Farmer & Rubber Chicken

Rubber Chicken: Hey, Farmer, why does your son cluck like a chicken?

Funny Farmer: Because he thinks he's a chicken.

Rubber Chicken: Why don't you tell him he's not a chicken?

Funny Farmer: We need the eggs!

2

Rubber Chicken: Do you know who tells the best Rubber Chicken jokes?
Funny Farmer: Who?
Rubber Chicken: Comedi-HENS!

Funny Farmer: Hey, I heard you swallowed a nickel. How are you feeling?
Rubber Chicken: Well, there's been no change yet!

Rubber Birds

Rubber Chicken was in the yard one day, telling jokes to his best friend, Rubber Ducky ...

Rubber Chicken: You know, for a long time I couldn't lay eggs.
Rubber Ducky: How did you learn?
Rubber Chicken: The farmer showed me an EGG-xample!

Rubber Chicken: What do you call a bear with no shoes?
Rubber Ducky: What?
Rubber Chicken: BEAR-foot.

Rubber Chicken: How does a Rubber Chicken send mail?
Rubber Ducky: In a HEN-velope!

Rubber Chicken: What do you call a deer with no eyes?
Rubber Ducky: What?
Rubber Chicken: I have no-eye-deer!

A Rubber Chicken Riddle

Rubber Chicken said to the librarian, "Book, Book, Book!" So the librarian gave him a book.

Rubber Chicken walked out. But in a moment, he came right back. Again he went to the librarian and said, "Book, Book, Book!" So she gave him another book.

When he left this time, the librarian followed him. She watched him drop the book on a lily pad in front of a frog. Then she heard what the frog had to say, and it all made sense.

What did the frog say?

**Answer:
"Read it. Read it. Read it."**

Horse Talk

One day, Horse looked unhappy, so Rubber Chicken asked why.

Rubber Chicken: Hey, Horse, why the long face?
Horse: I think I'm getting a cold.
Rubber Chicken: I think you might be right.
Horse: Oh, how come?
Rubber Chicken: Well, you sound very HOARSE.

Horse: Why do cows wear bells?
Rubber Chicken: Because their horns are too quiet!

Silly Sailor Visits Funny Farmer

Silly Sailor: You know, the strangest thing happened. Yesterday, my cat's meow sounded terrible, but today he's been purring a beautiful song all day long.
Funny Farmer: How weird! What did you feed him this morning?
Silly Sailor: Tune-a-fish!

Silly Sailor: So, what do you think of rubber chicken eggs?
Funny Farmer: Well, I'll tell you one thing, they're not all they're cracked up to be!

Funny Farmer: For a while, we thought we could use the rubber chickens in baking.
Silly Sailor: Really? For what?
Funny Farmer: We thought they might be good for COOP-cakes!

Silly Sailor: I was shipwrecked once and had to live for weeks on a rubber chicken.
Funny Farmer: Weren't you afraid you'd fall off?

Funny Farmer: You know, we've been doing some work with scientists here at the Funny Farm.
Silly Sailor: What kind of work?
Funny Farmer: Well, we crossed a chicken with a cow.
Silly Sailor: What did you get?
Funny Farmer: ROOST beef!

Funny Farmer: We also tried crossing porcupines with balloons, but that didn't work.
Silly Sailor: How come?
Funny Farmer: All we got was POP!

Rubber Chicken Riddles

Riddle: Rubber Chicken had 5 apples and 7 friends. How can he share the apples between them all?

Answer: He can make apple pie.

Riddle: You're a bus driver, driving a busload of rubber chickens to school. At the first stop, 3 rubber chickens bounce on. At the second stop, 6 rubber ducks get on. At the third stop, 2 chickens and 1 duck bounce and squeak their way off the bus. At the fourth stop, every rubber bird gets off. The riddle is, what color are the bus driver's eyes?

Answer: Look in the mirror.

Riddle:
Rubber Chicken was having some friends over to the coop for dinner. This is the recipe he used: Throw out the outside. Cook the inside. Eat the outside. Throw out the inside.

What did he cook?

Answer: Corn on the cob.

Rubber Chicken Crossing

Rubber Chicken: Why did the rubber chicken cross the playground?
Professor Turkey: To get to the other SLIDE!

Rubber Chicken: Why did the turkey cross the road?
Professor Turkey: To prove he wasn't a chicken!

Rubber Chicken: Why did the rubber chicken stop in the middle of the road with an egg?
Professor Turkey: He wanted to lay it on the line!

12

Rubber Chicken: I once had a cousin who crossed the road, rolled in the dirt, then came back across the road again!

Professor Turkey: He sounds like a dirty double-crosser!

Rubber Chicken: That reminds me, why didn't the skeleton cross the road?

Professor Turkey: He didn't have the guts!

Rubber Chicken: Okay, Professor, why did the gum cross the road?

Professor Turkey: Why?

Rubber Chicken: Because it was stuck to my foot!

They're Funny and Silly!

Funny Farmer: I've got a riddle for you. What gets wet while it dries?
Silly Sailor: I don't know. What?
Funny Farmer: A towel!

Silly Sailor: Well, I've got one for you! How much does it cost a pirate to get his ear pierced?

Funny Farmer: I don't know. How much?

Silly Sailor: A buck-an-ear.

Funny Farmer: Why are fish easier to weigh than rubber chickens?

Silly Sailor: I don't know. Why?

Funny Farmer: Fish come with their own scales!

Sticky Rubber Chickens

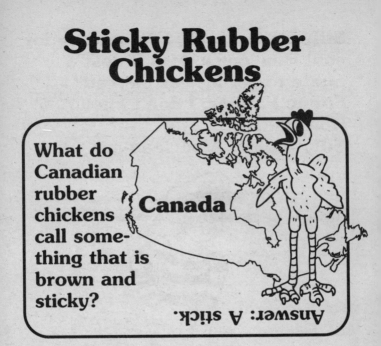

What do Canadian rubber chickens call something that is brown and sticky?

Canada

Answer: A stick.

What do Australian rubber chickens call a boomerang that won't come back?

Australia

Answer: A stick.

Rubbery Riddles

Riddle: Every day, Funny Farmer gives Rubber Chicken water out of something that is green and bucket-shaped. What is it?

Answer: A green bucket.

Riddle: A rubber chicken cowboy rode to a hotel on Friday, stayed there for two nights, and left on Friday. How could that be?

Answer: His horse's name was Friday.

Rubber Chicken Sports

Rubber Chicken: What do you call a rubber chicken basketball player?
Rubber Ducky: Beats me!
Rubber Chicken: Stretch!

Rubber Chicken: Why do rubber chickens make great basketball players?
Rubber Ducky: I don't know. Why?
Rubber Chicken: Because they always bounce back in the fourth quarter!

Rubber Chicken: Why did the rubber chicken cross the basketball court?
Rubber Ducky: I give up! Why?
Rubber Chicken: He heard the referee calling FOWLS!

18

Rubber Chicken's football team was ready to play in the big finals. Just before the game, the coach had to go to the bank. Can you guess why?

Answer: To get his quarter back.

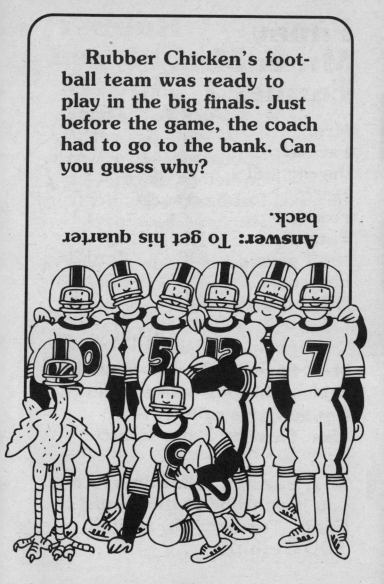

Funny Mr. & Mrs. Farmer

Mrs. Farmer: Is the pig still sick?
Funny Farmer: No, I gave him some OINK-ment!

Mrs. Farmer: Do you know how rubber chickens make cakes?
Funny Farmer: No. How?
Mrs. Farmer: From scratch!

Mrs. Farmer: What time to do you have to be at the dentist?
Funny Farmer: Oh, around TOOTH-thirty.

Funny Farmer: I went to market today and bought you a cow.

Mrs. Farmer: Why would I want a cow of my own?

Funny Farmer: Oh, this cow is special. It's an Arctic cow.

Mrs. Farmer: Why would I want an Arctic cow?

Funny Farmer: For cold cream!

Mrs. Farmer: Well, while you were gone, I counted all the cows. We have exactly 365, one for each day of the year.

Funny Farmer: It must have been hard to count all those cows.

Mrs. Farmer: No, it was easy. I used a COW-culator!

One day, some Canadian geese landed at the Funny Farm. Rubber Chicken invited them to stay for the winter, but they had to keep going south.

Rubber Chicken: Why do you fly south for the winter?
Goose: Because it's too far to walk.

Rubber Chicken: You know, yesterday I tried to fly in through that three-foot-high window, but I couldn't.

Goose: But you can fly almost four feet high. Why couldn't you fly through a three-foot-high window?

Rubber Chicken: It was closed.

Goose: You know, we met some strange birds on our travels. We met an owl that lost his voice!

Rubber Chicken: Was he upset?

Goose: No, he didn't give a hoot!

Rubber Chicken: That's nothing. Do you know what kind of bird is always out of breath?

Goose: No, what kind?

Rubber Chicken: A PUFFIN!

Conversations With Cow

Rubber Chicken: What do you call a sleeping bull?
Cow: What?
Rubber Chicken: A bulldozer!

Rubber Chicken: Why do rubber hens lay eggs?
Cow: I don't know. Why?
Rubber Chicken: Because if they dropped them, they'd break!

Rubber Chicken: You know, Rubber Ducky went out in the rain and didn't get a single hair on his head wet. Do you know how?
Cow: He had an umbrella?
Rubber Chicken: No, silly. Rubber duckies don't have hair.

Banker Ha-has

Banker: Hey, Funny Farmer. When is the best time to buy rubber chicks?

Funny Farmer: When they're going CHEEP!

Banker: What do you get when you cross a chicken with a cement mixer?

Funny Farmer: I don't know.

Banker: A bricklayer!

Funny Farmer: Why is six afraid of seven?

Banker: Why?

Funny Farmer: Because seven eight nine.

Egg-citing Rubber Chicken Jokes

What do rubber chickens grow on?

Answer: Eggplants!

How come rubber chickens are afraid of cakes?

Answer: Because cakes are full of beaten eggs!

What do rubber chickens get if they lay eggs on a hill?

Answer: An egg roll!

Here's a quiz that will make you scratch your egghead.

Take six glasses and put them in a row. Now, fill the first three glasses with water. The last three glasses should be empty.

Here's the quiz that gets Rubber Chicken's approval:

By moving only one glass, can you arrange them so that the full and empty glasses alternate?

Answer:
Pick up the second glass and pour the water into the fifth glass. Now, put the second glass back into the second position.

One day, while Rubber Chicken and Rubber Ducky were fishing, Rubber Chicken started feeling poetic. So, he came up with this poetic riddle for Ducky:

I run but never walk.
Have a mouth but never talk.
Have a bed but never lie.
What, do you think, am I?

Answer: A river!

Not one to be outdone, Rubber Ducky came right back with this:

I have no lungs, but I need air.
Though not alive, I grow.
I make a noise but have no mouth,
And hate only water and snow.

What was Ducky going on about?

Answer: Fire!

That same day, after fishing for a long time without one bite, Rubber Chicken and Rubber Ducky got to telling jokes about fish ...

Rubber Ducky: Why do fish live in saltwater?
Rubber Chicken: Because pepper makes them sneeze!

Rubber Ducky: Do you know what you'd get if you crossed two elephants with a fish?
Rubber Chicken: No. What?
Rubber Ducky: Swimming trunks!

Rubber Chicken: Maybe fish are just smarter than we are.
Rubber Ducky: Well, that makes sense.
Rubber Chicken: It does?
Rubber Ducky: Sure, they spend all their time in a school!

Funnies on the Farm

One day, Cow asked Rubber Chicken to tell some jokes. Rubber Chicken thought for a while, then remembered one. That started everyone in the farmyard telling funnies ...

Rubber Chicken: What do you get when you cross a rubber chicken with a centipede?
Cow: What?
Rubber Chicken: I don't know, but whatever it is, it tastes lousy, and everyone gets a leg.

Cow: Hey, Horse! Have you heard the joke about the two little snakes?

Horse: No, tell it to me.

Cow: There were two little snakes wiggling down the road. The smaller snake turned to the bigger snake and asked, "Are we poisonous?"

"Why?" asked the bigger one.

The little one replied, "Because I just bit my lip."

Horse: A pig's neck is so short. Why is a giraffe's neck so long?

Pig: I've heard it's because their feet smell awful!

Pig: What do you call a sheep with no legs?

Rubber Chicken: A cloud!

Here Comes That Silly Sailor Again!

Funny Farmer: You know, farming these rubber chickens is hard work!

Silly Sailor: Do you have to work long hours?

Funny Farmer: Oh yeah, I work around the CLUCK!

Silly Sailor: Do you ever take a day off?

Funny Farmer: Yep. Saturdays.

Silly Sailor: What do you do on Saturdays?

Funny Farmer: I take the rubber chickens out on a PECK-nic!

Funny Farmer: You know, I had to name my pig "Ink."

Silly Sailor: Whatever for?

Funny Farmer: He kept running out of his pen!

Silly Sailor: I've got a riddle that I'll draw in the dirt. It's an old saying. See if you can get it.

The Sailor took a stick and scratched this in the dirt by the pigpen:

T   I   M   E

abde

Answer: Long time, no see!

The Quarter Roll
An Official Rubber Chicken Practical Joke

First, find some ordinary fishing line or thread, about four or five feet long. Tape it to a piece of paper that says, "Top Secret." Or tape the thread to some paper money.

Now, call your mom or dad, then hide behind a piece of furniture or inside a doorway close by. Wait patiently for them to see the paper. Just when they reach down to pick it up, give the string a yank.

Watch your mom or dad jump with surprise. This one's sure to keep you amused for a while!

Banker: I'd like to buy one of your ducks.

Funny Farmer: They're $5.

Banker: Fine, just send me the bill.

Funny Farmer: I'm afraid I can't.

Banker: Why not?

Funny Farmer: You have to take the whole duck!

Funny Farmer: You know, Barber lost his dog in the woods.

Banker: Did he find it?

Funny Farmer: Yes. He just put his ear against a tree and listened to the bark!

Banker: Why is that crate of ducks over by the soup?

Funny Farmer: They're a box of quackers!

More Conversations with Cow ...

Cow: Why does your chicken coop have only two doors?
Rubber Chicken: If it had four doors, it would be a sedan.

Cow: You know, I've always wondered where we cows come from.

Rubber Chicken: To find out, you should go to the MOO-seum!

Cow: Why did the cow cross the road?

Rubber Chicken: Why?

Cow: To get to the UDDER side!

Cow: What do you get when you cross a clumsy rubber chicken with a cow?

Rubber Chicken: Butterfingers!

Cow: I've got a date tonight.

Rubber Chicken: Where are you going?

Cow: Where else? I'm going to the MOO-vies!

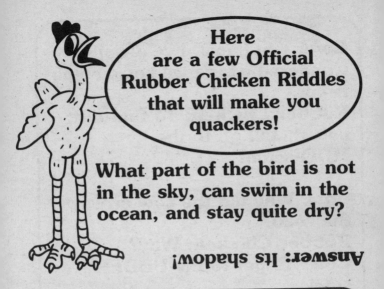

Here are a few Official Rubber Chicken Riddles that will make you quackers!

What part of the bird is not in the sky, can swim in the ocean, and stay quite dry?

Answer: Its shadow!

What are these things on the Funny Farm?

They come at night without being called and are lost in the day without being stolen.

Answer: Stars!

What goes up when the rain comes down?

Answer: An umbrella!

Rabbit Trouble

Funny Farmer was fixing the fence to keep the rabbits in, when the barber stopped by.

Barber: What are you doing?

Funny Farmer: Well, yesterday, there was a line of a hundred rabbits outside this fence.

Barber: And you think this fence will keep them out?

Funny Farmer: I'm hoping it will keep them back.

Barber: You're the first man I've ever met who was hoping for a receding hare line!

Funny Farmer: I tried another treatment, but it didn't work.

Barber: What did you do?

Funny Farmer: I poured hot water down all the rabbit holes.

Barber: And it didn't work?

Funny Farmer: No, I just ended up with hot, cross bunnies!

Conversations with Horse

Rubber Chicken: If apes live in trees, where do they sleep?
Horse: In apricots!

Rubber Chicken: You know, Rubber Ducky lost his voice the other day.
Horse: Really?
Rubber Chicken: Yes. At first I thought he was giving me the silent TWEET-ment.

Rubber Chicken: I have a cousin who mocks everything I say.
Horse: Don't you get angry?
Rubber Chicken: No, it's not his fault. He's a mockingbird.

Rubber Chicken: I have a bird friend who spends all his time underground.
Horse: What kind of bird is he?
Rubber Chicken: He's a MYNAH (miner).

Horse: That reminds me. What do you get when you throw a piano down a mineshaft?
Rubber Chicken: What?
Horse: A flat miner!

Rubber Chicken: You know, my grandfather was in the war.
Rubber Ducky: Really?
Rubber Chicken: Yes. He was almost injured.
Rubber Ducky: What happened?
Rubber Chicken: A HEN-grenade eggs-ploded right next to him.

Rubber Ducky: Well, my grandfather was also in the war.
Rubber Chicken: Really?
Rubber Ducky: Yes, he was in the airborne regiment and his SPARROW-chute didn't open!

Rubber Ducky: I've got a riddle for you.

Rubber Chicken: Shoot!

Rubber Ducky: What occurs once a minute, twice a moment, but never in a thousand years?

Rubber Chicken: That's a tricky one. I don't know.

Rubber Ducky: The letter M.

Rubber Ducky: Rubber chickens are always standing and sitting and they hardly ever fly. Are there any kinds of birds that only kneel?

Rubber Chicken: Sure!

Rubber Ducky: What kind?

Rubber Chicken: Birds of PREY (pray)!

43

Quarter Roll

**An Official
Rubber Chicken
Practical Joke**

All you need is a
piece of paper, two
quarters, and a
pencil.

Tell a friend that you're going to
test his or her coordination. Place
one quarter on the paper and run
the pencil around it several times,
drawing a circle. This will coat the
outside of the quarter with lead
from the pencil.

Now, tell your friend that the trick
is to roll the quarter from one's
chin to forehead and then place the
quarter on the circle. You can
demonstrate on yourself with the
clean quarter.

The result? Your friend will have a
long black line running from chin
to forehead, and you won't!

Quarter Roll

Rubber Chicken wanted to give Rubber Rooster something special.

Rubber Chicken: I need to find an extra-special present for Dad.

Cow: How come?

Rubber Chicken: Today is Feather's day!

Cow: Hmmm. Are there any foods that he likes?

Rubber Chicken: Every morning he has a bowl of cereal.

Cow: What kind?

Rubber Chicken: Shredded TWEET!

The Funny Farm Ball

Horse: What do you call a dance for rubber chickens and rubber ducks?
Rubber Ducky: What?
Horse: A Rubber Ball!

Rubber Ducky: What a coincidence! I'm off to a ball.
Horse: Are you wearing anything special?
Rubber Ducky: Yes, my squeaky-clean DUCK-seedo!

Rubber Chicken: Of course, Rubber Ducky won't be doing any slow dances.
Horse: Why?
Rubber Chicken: He prefers the QUACKstep (quickstep).

Rubber Chicken: I hear that the musicians are all bison.
Cow: Yes, they've got a fantastic HORN section.
Rubber Chicken: Did they all come together in one big truck?
Cow: Yes. The BUFFO-LOAD arrive this afternoon.

Rubber Chicken: And did I hear, Cow, that the bull will be singing tonight?
Cow (blushing): Yes, he'll be singing "When I fall in love, it will be for-HEIFER!"

Last Words on Rubber Chickens

What did Rubber Chicken say when he saw his mother sitting on an orange?

Answer: "Look at what Marmalade (*Mama laid*)!"

Why do rubber roosters have it harder than rubber chickens?

Answer: They have to get up at the QUACK of dawn!

Why did the rubber chicken cross the internet?

Answer: To get to the other SITE!